THE EASY G MAJOR FAKE BOOK

Melody, Lyrics and Simplified Ch[ords]

Over 100 Songs · THE · In the Key of "G"

THE EASY G MAJOR FAKE BOOK

ISBN 978-1-4950-1151-1

HAL•LEONARD®
CORPORATION

7777 W. BLUEMOUND RD. P.O. BOX 13819 MILWAUKEE, WI 53213

Visit Hal Leonard Online at
www.halleonard.com

THE EASY G MAJOR FAKE BOOK

CONTENTS

INTRODUCTION

What Is a Fake Book?

A fake book has one-line music notation consisting of melody, lyrics and chord symbols. This lead sheet format is a "musical shorthand" which is an invaluable resource for all musicians—hobbyists to professionals.

Here's how *The Easy G Major Fake Book* differs from most standard fake books:

- All songs are in the key of G.

- Many of the melodies have been simplified.

- Only five basic chord types are used—major, minor, seventh, diminished and augmented.

- The music notation is larger for ease of reading.

In the event that you haven't used chord symbols to create accompaniment, or your experience is limited, a chord speller chart is included at the back of the book to help you get started.

Have fun!

ABILENE

Words and Music by LESTER BROWN,
JOHN D. LOUDERMILK and BOB GIBSON

AGAINST THE WIND

Words and Music by
BOB SEGER

ALL I HAVE TO DO IS DREAM

Words and Music by
BOUDLEAUX BRYANT

ALL RIGHT NOW

Words and Music by ANDY FRASER
and PAUL RODGERS

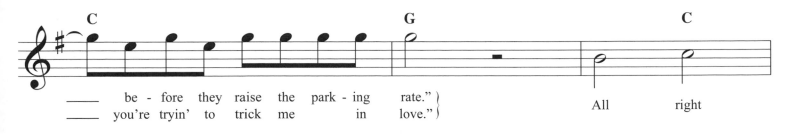

_____ be - fore they raise the park - ing rate." }
_____ you're tryin' to trick me in love." }
All right

now, _____ ba - by, it's all _____ right _____ now.

All right now, _____ ba - by, it's all _____ right _____

1
now.

2
I took her now.

All right now, _____ ba - by, it's all _____

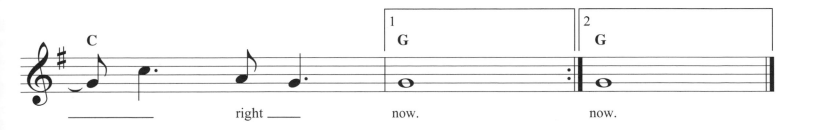

_____ right _____ now.

1

2
now.

BABY, I LOVE YOUR WAY

Words and Music by
PETER FRAMPTON

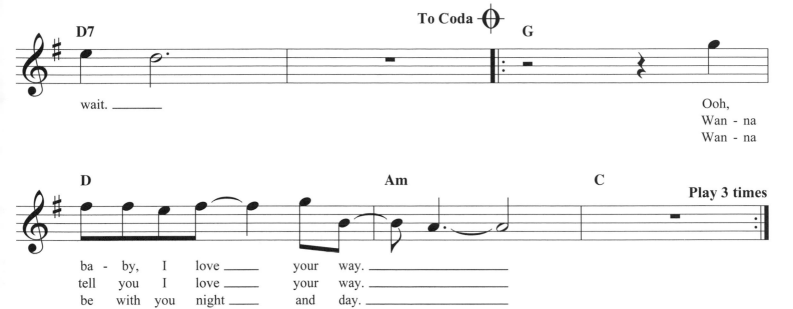

wait. _____

Ooh,
Wan - na
Wan - na

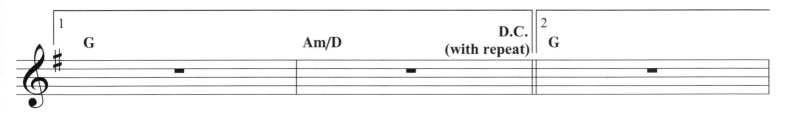

ba - by, I love _____ your way. _____
tell you I love _____ your way. _____
be with you night _____ and day. _____

Play 3 times

D.S. al Coda

But

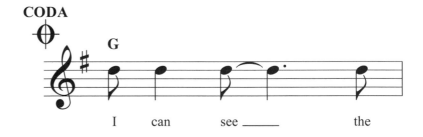

CODA

I can see _____ the

sun - set in your eyes, _____ brown and

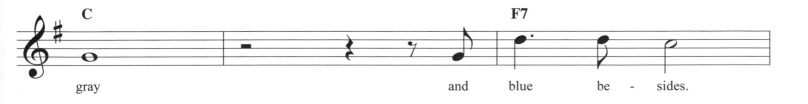

gray and blue be - sides.

Clouds are stalk - ing is - lands in the sun. _____

American Pie

Words and Music by
DON McLEAN

Freely

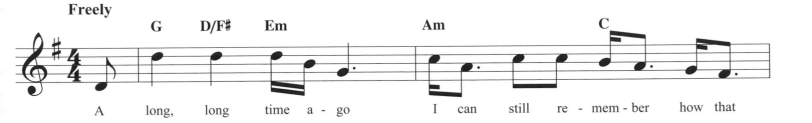

A long, long time a-go I can still re-mem-ber how that

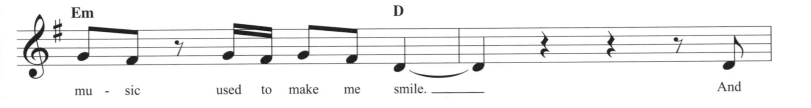

mu - sic used to make me smile. _____ And

I knew if I had my chance that I could make those peo - ple dance and

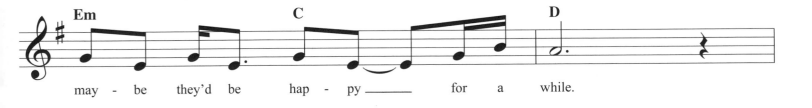

may - be they'd be hap - py _____ for a while.

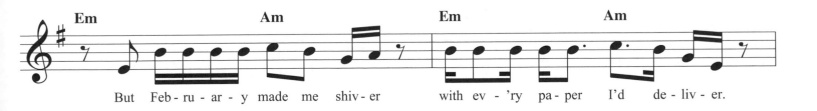

But Feb-ru-ar-y made me shiv - er with ev - 'ry pa-per I'd de-liv-er.

Bad news on the door-step, I could-n't take one more step. I

can't re-mem-ber if I cried when I read a-bout his wid-owed bride.

Some-thing touched me deep in-side _____ the day the mu-sic died. _____

Moderately

_____ So bye-bye Miss A-mer-i-can Pie _____ drove my

Chev-y to the lev-ee but the lev-ee was dry. ___ Them good ole boys ___ were drink-in'

To Coda

whis-key and rye, ___ sing-in' this-'ll be the day ___ that I _____ die.

17

This - 'll be the day ___ that I ___ die. ___

{ 1. Did you ___ write the book of love ___ and do you _
{ 2.–4. *(See additional lyrics)*

___ have faith in God a - bove? _   If the Bi - ble tells _

___ you so. ___   Now do you ___ be - lieve ___ in

rock and roll? ___ Can mu - sic save your mor - tal soul ___ and

can you teach me how to dance ___ real slow? ___

she just smiled ___ and turned a - way. _____

I went down to the sa - cred store _____ where I heard the mu - sic years be - fore, but the

man there said the mu - sic would - n't play. _____ And

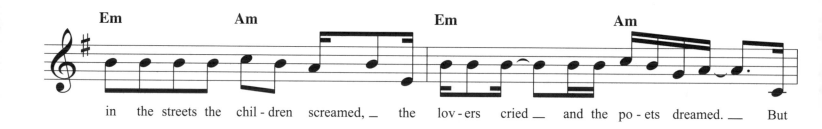

in the streets the chil - dren screamed, _ the lov - ers cried _ and the po - ets dreamed. _ But

not a word was spo - ken, the church bells all were bro - ken. And the three men I ad - mire most, the

Fa - ther, Son and the Ho - ly Ghost, they caught the last train for the coast the

day the mu - sic died. And they were sing - in'

CODA

this - 'll be the day ___ that I ___ die. ___

2. Now for ten years we've been on our own,
And moss grows fat on a rollin' stone
But that's not how it used to be
When the jester sang for the king and queen
In a coat he borrowed from James Dean
And a voice that came from you and me
Oh and while the king was looking down,
The jester stole his thorny crown
The courtroom was adjourned,
No verdict was returned
And while Lenin read a book on Marx
The quartet practiced in the park
And we sang dirges in the dark
The day the music died
We were singin'...bye-bye... etc.

3. Helter-skelter in the summer swelter
The birds flew off with a fallout shelter
Eight miles high and fallin' fast,
It landed foul on the grass
The players tried for a forward pass,
With the jester on the sidelines in a cast
Now the half-time air was sweet perfume
While the sergeants played a marching tune
We all got up to dance
But we never got the chance
'Cause the players tried to take the field,
The marching band refused to yield
Do you recall what was revealed
The day the music died
We started singin'... bye-bye...etc.

4. And there we were all in one place,
A generation lost in space
With no time left to start again
So come on, Jack be nimble, Jack be quick,
Jack Flash sat on a candlestick
'Cause fire is the devil's only friend
And as I watched him on the stage
My hands were clenched in fits of rage
No angel born in hell
Could break that Satan's spell
And as the flames climbed high into the night
To light the sacrificial rite
I saw Satan laughing with delight
The day the music died
He was singin'...bye-bye...etc.

BEAUTIFUL IN MY EYES

Words and Music by
JOSHUA KADISON

(It's A)
BEAUTIFUL MORNING

Words and Music by FELIX CAVALIERE
and EDWARD BRIGATI, JR.

BEST OF MY LOVE

Words and Music by JOHN DAVID SOUTHER,
DON HENLEY and GLENN FREY

BEAUTY AND THE BEAST
from Walt Disney's BEAUTY AND THE BEAST

Music by ALAN MENKEN
Lyrics by HOWARD ASHMAN

CALIFORNIA, HERE I COME

Words and Music by AL JOLSON
B.G. DeSYLVA and JOSEPH MEYER

CROCODILE ROCK

Words and Music by ELTON JOHN
and BERNIE TAUPIN

_____ I nev - er _____ will. _____ Oh, _____

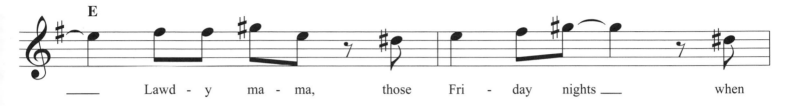

_____ Lawd - y ma - ma, those Fri - day nights _____ when

Su - sie wore _____ her dress - es tight _____ and

the croc - o - dile _____ rock - in' was _____ out of

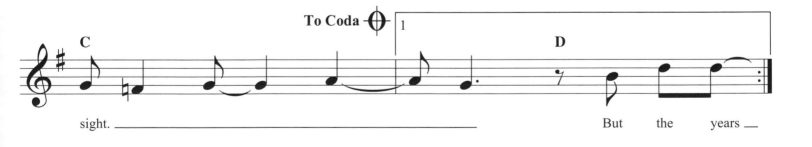

sight. _____ But the years _____

_____ I re - mem -

CLOSER TO FREE

Words and Music by SAM LLANAS
and KURT NEUMANN

DO NOTHIN' TILL YOU HEAR FROM ME

Words and Music by DUKE ELLINGTON
and BOB RUSSELL

Do noth-in' till you hear from me.
me.   At least con-sid-er our ro-

Pay no at-ten-tion to what's

said,   why peo-ple tear the seam of an-y-one's dream ____
mance;   if you should take the word of oth-ers you've heard, ____

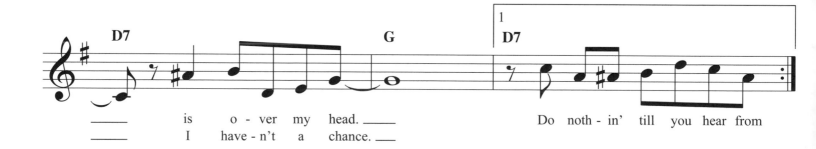

____ is o-ver my head. ____
____ I have-n't a chance. ____

Do noth-in' till you hear from

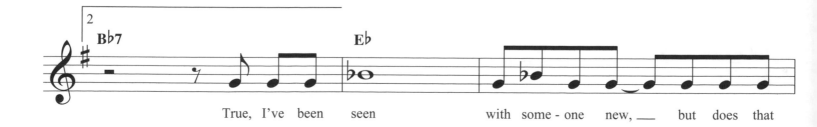

True, I've been seen   with some-one new, __ but does that

D7

mean that I'm un - true? ___ When we're a - part, _____ the

G   E7   D   A7

words in my heart ___ re - veal how I feel ___ a - bout you. ___

D7   G   G7

___ Some kiss may cloud my mem - o - ry, and oth - er arms may hold a

C   F7   G   Am

thrill. But please do noth - in' till you hear it from me _____

D7   G

___ and you nev - er will. _____

(Sittin' On)
THE DOCK OF THE BAY

Words and Music by STEVE CROPPER
and OTIS REDDING

DREAM LOVER

Words and Music by
BOBBY DARIN

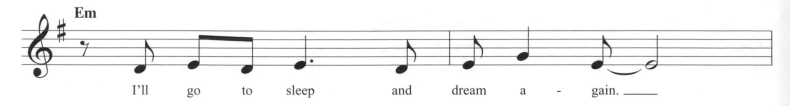

I'll go to sleep and dream a - gain. ____

That's the on - ly thing to do ____

un - til my lov - er's dreams come true. ____ Be - cause I

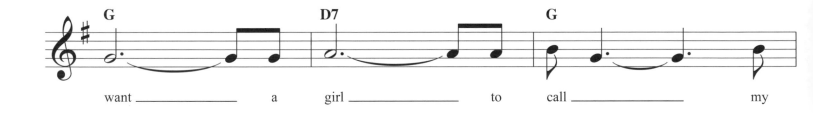

want ____ a girl ____ to call ____ my

own, ____ I want a dream lov - er so

I don't have to dream a - lone. ____

A DREAM IS A WISH YOUR HEART MAKES
from Walt Disney's CINDERELLA

Words and Music by MACK DAVID,
AL HOFFMAN and JERRY LIVINGSTON

Moderately

G

A dream is a wish your heart makes _____ when you're

B7   C   E7   Am

fast a - sleep. _____ In dreams you will lose your heart - aches; _

D7   G   D7   G

_ what - ev - er you wish for, you keep. Have faith in your

G7

dreams and some - day _____ your rain - bow will come smil - ing

C   Am   F7   G

thru. _____ No mat - ter how your heart is griev - ing, if you keep on be -

A7   D7   G

liev - ing, the dream that you wish will come true. _____

EASY TO LOVE
(You'd Be So Easy to Love)
from BORN TO DANCE

Words and Music by
COLE PORTER

EMBRACEABLE YOU
from CRAZY FOR YOU

Music and Lyrics by GEORGE GERSHWIN
and IRA GERSHWIN

EIGHT DAYS A WEEK

Words and Music by JOHN LENNON
and PAUL McCARTNEY

(*Instrumental*)

EVERY ROSE HAS ITS THORN

Words and Music by BOBBY DALL,
C.C. DEVILLE, BRET MICHAELS
and RIKKI ROCKETT

ev - 'ry cow - boy _____ sings his sad, sad _____ song,

ev - 'ry rose has its thorn.

I thorn.

Though it's been a - while _ now I can still feel so much pain. _

Like the knife that cuts _ you, the wound heals, but the scar, that scar re -

mains.

I know I could have saved our love that night _ if I'd

known what to say. ___ In - stead of mak - ing love ___ we both

made our sep -'rate ways. ___ Now I hear you've found some - bod - y new ___ and

that I nev - er meant that much to you. ___ To hear that tears me up in - side ___ and to

see you cuts me like a knife. I guess ev - 'ry rose has its

thorn, just like ev - 'ry night has its dawn. _____ Just like

ev - 'ry cow - boy _____ sings his sad, sad ___ song,

ev - 'ry rose has its thorn.

FOR ALL WE KNOW

Words by SAM M. LEWIS
Music by J. FRED COOTS

THE FIRST CUT IS THE DEEPEST

Words and Music by
CAT STEVENS

G　　　　　**D**　　　　　**C**　　　　　**D**

The first cut is the deep - est; ba - by, I know ___

G　　　　　**D**　　　　　**C**　　　　　**D**

___ the first cut is the deep - est. When it

G　　　　　**D**　　　　　**C**　　　　　**D**

comes to be - in' luck - y she's cursed. ___ When it

1
G　　　　　**C**　　　　　**D**

comes to lov - in' me she's worse. ___ I still

2
G　　　　　**D**　　　　　**C**　　　　　**G**

comes to lov - in' me she's worse. ___

FREE BIRD

Words and Music by ALLEN COLLINS
and RONNIE VAN ZANT

GETTING TO KNOW YOU
from THE KING AND I

Lyrics by OSCAR HAMMERSTEIN II
Music by RICHARD RODGERS

get - ting to feel free and eas - y. _____ When I am

with you, get - ting to know what to say. _____

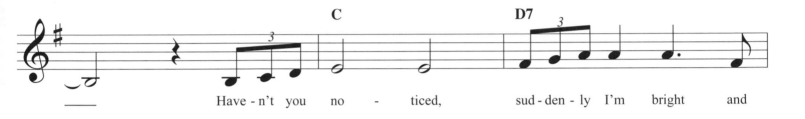

____ Have - n't you no - ticed, sud - den - ly I'm bright and

breez - y, _____ be - cause of all the

beau - ti - ful and new things I'm learn - ing a - bout you

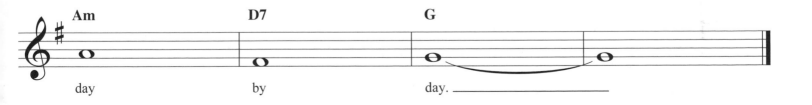

day by day. _____

GOT TO GET YOU INTO MY LIFE

Words and Music by JOHN LENNON
and PAUL McCARTNEY

day   of my   life? _____
geth - er ev - 'ry   day. _____
day   of my   life? _____

Got   to get you in - to my   life! ____ *(Instrumental)*

Got   to get you in - to my   life! ____ *(Instrumental)*

Got to get you in - to my   life! __

____ *(Instrumental)*

A GROOVY KIND OF LOVE

Words and Music by TONI WINE
and CAROLE BAYER SAGER

When I'm feel-in' blue, all I have to do is take a look at you, then I'm not so

blue. When you're close to me, I can feel your heart beat. I can hear you

breath - ing in my ear. Would-n't you a - gree? Ba - by, you and

me got a groov-y kind of love. We got a groov-y kind of love.

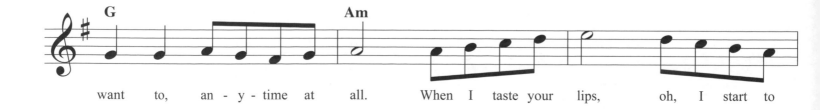

An - y - time you want to, you can turn me on to an - y - thing you

want to, an - y - time at all. When I taste your lips, oh, I start to

HARD TO SAY I'M SORRY

Words and Music by PETER CETERA
and DAVID FOSTER

FOREVER AND EVER, AMEN

Words and Music by PAUL OVERSTREET
and DON SCHLITZ

you a-gain. this song ends. I'm gon-na love____ you for-ev-er and ev-

-er, for-ev-er and ev-er, a-men.

(Instrumental)

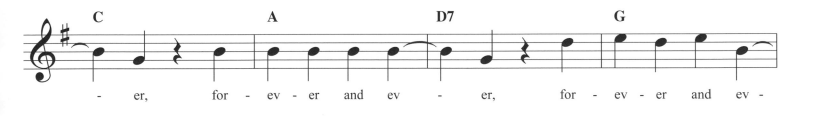

They say I'm gon-na love____ you for-ev-er and ev-

-er, for-ev-er and ev-er, for-ev-er and ev-

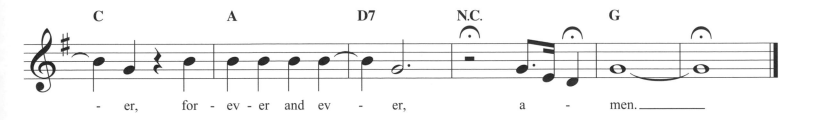

-er, for-ev-er and ev-er, a-men.____

HE STOPPED LOVING HER TODAY

Words and Music by BOBBY BRADDOCK
and CURLY PUTMAN

Additional Lyrics

3. *(Spoken:)* You know, she came to see him one last time.
We all wondered if she would.
And it came running through my mind,
This time he's over her for good.
Chorus

(Everything I Do)
I DO IT FOR YOU
from the Motion Picture ROBIN HOOD: PRINCE OF THIEVES

Words and Music by BRYAN ADAMS,
R.J. LANGE and MICHAEL KAMEN

tell me it's not worth dy-in' for. }
help it, there's noth-in' I want more. }
You know it's

true, _____ ev-'ry-thing I do, I do it for __ you.

There's no love like your love and no

oth-er could give more ____ love. There's no - where _____ un-less

you're there all the time, _____ all the way, __ yeah. _____

____ (Instrumental)

Oh, you can't tell me it's not worth try - in'

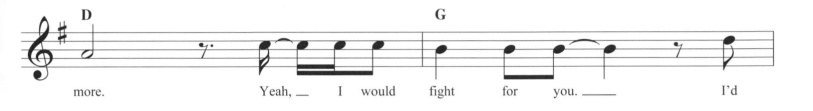

for.   I can't help _____ it, there's noth - in' I want

more.   Yeah, _ I would fight for you. _____ I'd

lie _____ for you, _ walk the wire for you, _ yeah, _ I'd

die for _ you. _ You know it's true, ev - 'ry - thing I

do,   oh, _____ I do it for _ you.

HERE, THERE AND EVERYWHERE

Words and Music by JOHN LENNON
and PAUL McCARTNEY

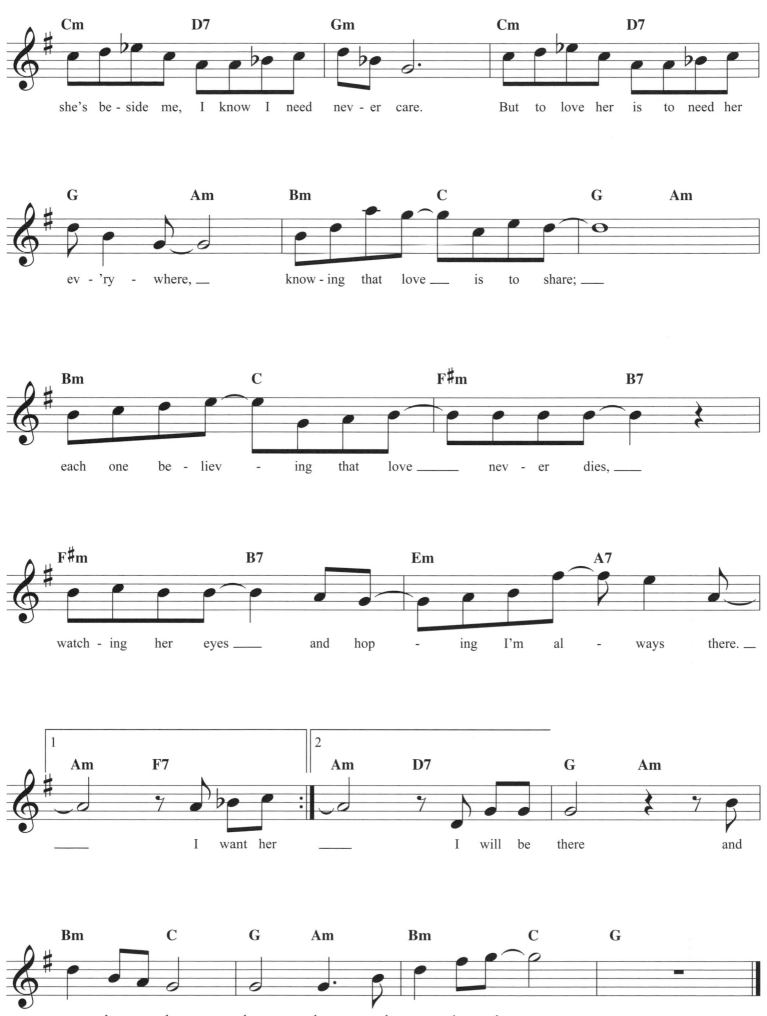

HERO

Words and Music by MARIAH CAREY
and WALTER AFANASIEFF

HEY THERE
from THE PAJAMA GAME

Words and Music by RICHARD ADLER
and JERRY ROSS

I'LL BE

Words and Music by
EDWIN McCAIN

trap - pings of ____ love. _____ I'll be ____ cap - ti -

vat - ed, I'll hang ____ from your ____ lips in -

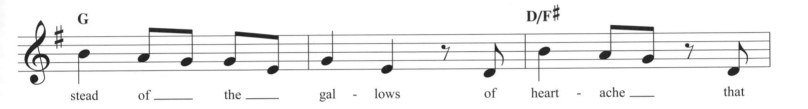

stead of ____ the ____ gal - lows of heart - ache ____ that

hang from a - bove. _____

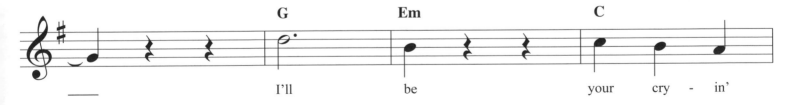

____ I'll be your cry - in'

shoul - der. ____ I'll ____ be ____ love

I'LL BE SEEING YOU
from RIGHT THIS WAY

Written by IRVING KAHAL
and SAMMY FAIN

Slowly

I'll be see-ing you in all the old fa-mil-iar plac-es
that this heart of mine em-brac-es all day through.
In that small ca-fé, the park a-cross the way, the
chil-dren's ca-rou-sel, the chest-nut trees, the wish-ing well.
I'll be see-ing you in ev-'ry love-ly sum-mer's day, in
ev-'ry-thing that's light and gay, I'll al-ways think of you that way I'll
find you in the morn-ing sun, and when the night is new, I'll be
look-ing at the moon, _____ but I'll be see-ing you! _____

I'M SO LONESOME I COULD CRY

Words and Music by
HANK WILLIAMS

I'M A BELIEVER

Words and Music by
NEIL DIAMOND

liev - er! I could - n't leave her if I tried.

(Instrumental)

CODA

Saw her face; _____ now I'm a be -

liev - er! Not a trace _____

of doubt __ in my mind. _____ I'm in love, _____

and I'm a be - liev - er! I'm in

IF MY FRIENDS COULD SEE ME NOW
from SWEET CHARITY

Music by CY COLEMAN
Lyrics by DOROTHY FIELDS

chums I at - tract. _____ All I can say is "Wow -
three kinds of fur." _____ All I can say is, "Wow! _
oth - er half lives." _____ To think the high - est brow, _

- ee! Look - a where I am. _____ To - night I
_____ Wait till the riff and raff _____ see just ex -
_____ which I must say is he, _____ should pick the

land - ed, pow, _____ right in a pot of jam." ___
act - ly how _____ he signed his au - to - graph." _
low - est brow, _____ which there's no doubt is me. ____

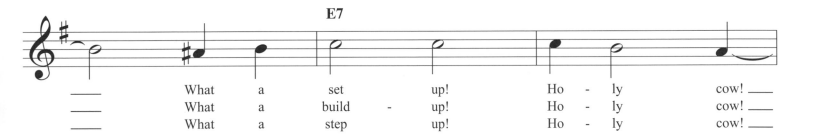

_____ What a set up! Ho - ly cow! ___
_____ What a build - up! Ho - ly cow! ___
_____ What a step up! Ho - ly cow! ___

_____ } They'd nev - er be - lieve it, if my friends could

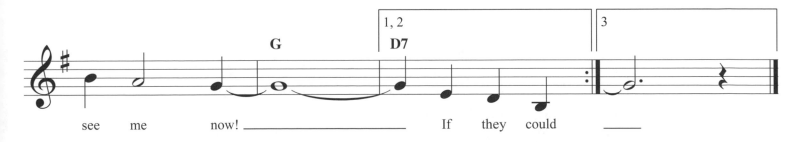

see me now! _____ If they could _____

IF YOU LEAVE ME NOW

Words and Music by
PETER CETERA

Moderately slow

If you leave me now,___ you'll take a - way the big - gest part___
leave me now,___ you'll take a - way the ver - y heart___

___ of me.___
___ of me.___
Oh,_____ no,___ ba - by, please___

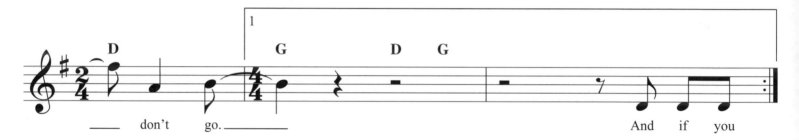

___ don't go._____
And if you

___ Oh,_____ girl,___ I just want you to stay.___

___
A love
We've come___

___ like ours___ is love___ that's hard___ to find._____
___ too far___ to leave___ it all___ be - hind._____

How could we let _____ it ____ slip ____ a - way? ____
How could we end _____ it ____ all ____ this way? ____

_____ _____ When to - mor -

- row comes, __ then we'll both _____ re - gret __ the things we said ___ to - day. __

_____ (Instrumental)

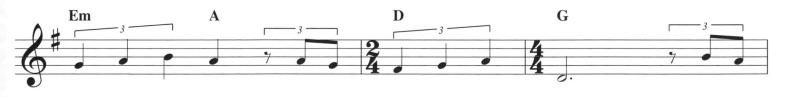

D.S. al Coda
(with repeat)

CODA

If you leave me now, ____ you'll

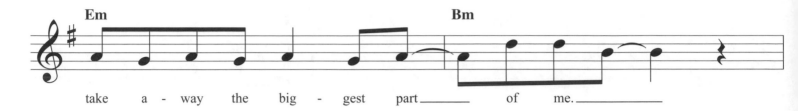

take a - way the big - gest part ____ of me. ____

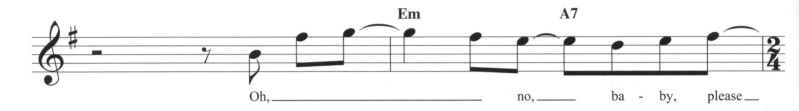

Oh, _____ no, ____ ba - by, please __

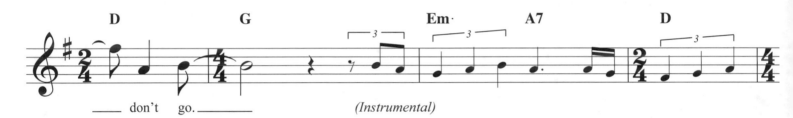

__ don't go. _____ *(Instrumental)*

Oh, _____ girl, ____ just got to have __ you by

my side. _____ *(Instrumental)*

IT'S A SMALL WORLD

from Disneyland Resort® and Magic Kingdom® Park

Words and Music by RICHARD M. SHERMAN
and ROBERT B. SHERMAN

IN THE MOOD

By JOE GARLAND

Moderate Swing

IT HAD TO BE YOU

Words by GUS KAHN
Music by ISHAM JONES

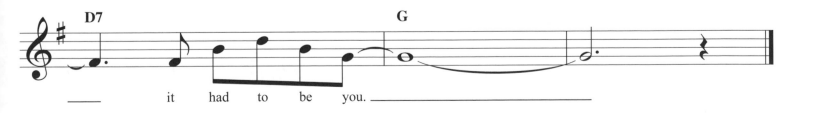

JAILHOUSE ROCK

Words and Music by JERRY LEIBER
and MIKE STOLLER

Additional Lyrics

2. Spider Murphy played the tenor saxophone,
   Little Joe was blowin' on the slide trombone,
   The drummer boy from Illinois went crash, boom, bang;
   The whole rhythm section was the Purple Gang.
   Chorus

3. Number Forty-seven said to number Three:
   "You're the cutest jailbird I ever did see.
   I sure would be delighted with your company,
   Come on and do the Jailhouse Rock with me."
   Chorus

4. The sad sack was a-sittin' on a block of stone,
   Way over in the corner weeping all alone.
   The warden said: "Hey, Buddy, don't you be so square.
   If you can't find a partner, use a wooden chair!"
   Chorus

5. Shifty Henry said to Bugs: "For heaven's sake,
   No one's lookin', now's our chance to make a break."
   Bugsy turned to Shifty and he said: "Nix, nix;
   I wanna stick around a while and get my kicks."
   Chorus

KNOCK THREE TIMES

Words and Music by IRWIN LEVINE
and LARRY RUSSELL BROWN

LA BAMBA

By RITCHIE VALENS

LEARNING TO FLY

Words and Music by TOM PETTY
and JEFF LYNNE

103

LET'S GO FLY A KITE
from Walt Disney's MARY POPPINS

Words and Music by RICHARD M. SHERMAN
and ROBERT B. SHERMAN

LEAVING ON A JET PLANE

Words and Music by
JOHN DENVER

(Instrumental)

LONGER

Words and Music by
DAN FOGELBERG

(Instrumental)

Long - er than there've been

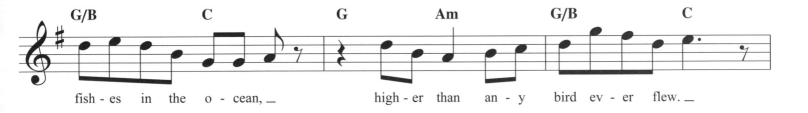

fish - es in the o - cean, ___ high - er than an - y bird ev - er flew. ___

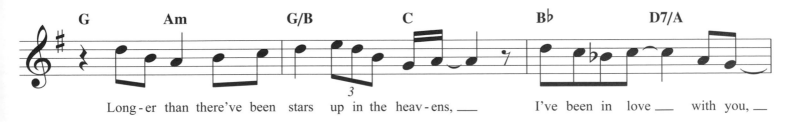

Long - er than there've been stars up in the heav - ens, ___ I've been in love ___ with you, ___

___ I am in love ___ with you. _____

LOVE ME TENDER

Words and Music by ELVIS PRESLEY
and VERA MATSON

MAGGIE MAY

Words and Music by ROD STEWART
and MARTIN QUITTENTON

(Instrumental)

Additional Lyrics

3. All I needed was a friend
   To lend a guiding hand.
   But you turned into a lover, and, mother, what a lover!
   You wore me out.
   All you did was wreck my bed,
   And, in the morning, kick me in the head.
   Oh, Maggie, I couldn't have tried any more.
   You led me away from home
   'Cause you didn't want to be alone.
   You stole my heart. I couldn't leave you if I tried.

4. I suppose I could collect my books
   And get on back to school.
   Or steal my daddy's cue
   And make a living out of playing pool.
   Or find myself a rock 'n roll band
   That needs a helping hand.
   Oh, Maggie, I wish I'd never seen your face.
   You made a first-class fool out of me.
   But I'm as blind as a fool can be.
   You stole my heart, but I love you anyway.

MY BOYFRIEND'S BACK

Words and Music by ROBERT FELDMAN,
GERALD GOLDSTEIN and RICHARD GOTTEHRER

Moderately

My boy-friend's back, and you're gon-na be in trou-ble.
He's been gone for such a long time.

(Hey, la-di-la, my boy-friend's back.)

When you see him com-in', bet-ter
Now he's back and

(Hey, la-di-la, my boy friend's back)

cut out on the dou-ble.
things will be fine.

You're

You've been spread-in' lies that I was un-true.
gon-na be sor-ry you ev-er were born.

(Hey, la-di-

la, my boy-friend's back.)

So look out now 'cause he's com-in' af-ter you.
'Cause he's kind of big and he's aw-ful strong.

(Hey, la-di-la, my boy-friend's back.)

And _____ he
And _____ he

THE NIGHT THEY DROVE OLD DIXIE DOWN

Words and Music by
ROBBIE ROBERTSON

1. Vir - gil Caine ___ is my name ___ and I drove on the Dan - ville train, ___

2., 3. *(See additional lyrics)*

___ 'til Stone - man's cav - al - ry came ___ and

tore up the tracks a - gain. _____ In the win - ter of six -

ty - five, we were hun - gry, ___ just ___ bare - ly a - live. ___

By May the tenth the Rich - mond had fell; ___ it was a time I re -

mem - ber, oh, ___ so well. ___ The night ___

Chorus

they drove old Dix - ie down ____ and all the

bells were ring - ing. The night they drove old Dix - ie down __

____ and all the peo - ple were sing - ing. They went: Na na na

na na na, ____ na na na na na na ____ na na ____ na.

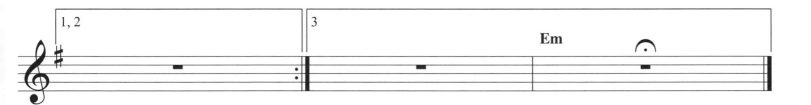

Additional Lyrics

2. Back with my wife in Tennessee, and one day she said to me,
   "Virgil, quick, come see. There goes Robert E. Lee."
   Now I don't mind, I'm chopping wood,
   And I don't care if the money's no good.
   Just take what you need and leave the rest,
   But they should never have taken the very best.
   Chorus

3. Like my father before me, I'm a working man.
   And like my brother before me, I took a rebel stand.
   But he was just eighteen, proud and brave,
   But a Yankee laid him in his grave.
   I swear by the blood below my feet,
   You can't raise a Caine back up when he's in defeat.
   Chorus

NINE TO FIVE

Words and Music by
DOLLY PARTON

NORWEGIAN WOOD
(This Bird Has Flown)

Words and Music by JOHN LENNON
and PAUL McCARTNEY

round and I no-ticed there was-n't a chair. ____

did-n't and crawled off to sleep in the bath. ____

____

____ I sat on a

And when I a-

rug, bid-ing my time, drink-ing her

woke I was a-lone; this bird had

wine. ____ We talked un-til

flown. ____ So I lit a

two and then she said, "It's time for

fire, is-n't it good, Nor-we-gian

1 bed." ____

2 wood? ____

ON A CLEAR DAY
(You Can See Forever)
from ON A CLEAR DAY YOU CAN SEE FOREVER

Words by ALAN JAY LERNER
Music by BURTON LANE

ONLY THE LONELY
(Know the Way I Feel)

Words and Music by ROY ORBISON
and JOE MELSON

Moderately

On - ly the lone - ly know the way I feel to - night. _____
lone - ly know the heart - aches I've been through. _____

_____ On - ly the lone - ly know this feel - ing ain't right. _____
_____ On - ly the lone - ly know I cry and cry for you. _____

_____ There goes my ba - by. _____ There goes my
_____ May - be to - mor - row, _____ a new ro -

heart. _____ They've gone for - ev - er _____ so far a -
mance, _____ no more sor - row. _____ But that's the

part. _____ But on - ly the lone - ly _____ know _____
chance _____ you've got to take if you're _____ lone -

why _____ I cry. _____ On - ly the
ly, _____ heart - break. _____ On - ly the

1.
lone - ly. _____ On - ly the

2.
lone - ly. _____

ONLY YOU
(And You Alone)

Words and Music by BUCK RAM
and ANDE RAND

PEACE OF MIND

Words and Music by
TOM SCHOLZ

Moderate Rock

Now, if you're feel - in' kind - a low 'bout the dues you've been pay - in',
climb - in' to the top of the com - pa - ny lad - der,
bod - y's got ad - vice they just keep on giv - in',

fu - ture's com - in' much too _____ slow, _____ and you
hope it does - n't take too _____ long. _____ Can't you
does - n't mean too much to me. _____

wan - na run but some - how you just keep on stay - in',
see there'll come a day when it won't mat - ter,
Lots of peo - ple have to make be - lieve they're liv - in';

can't de - cide on which way to go. _____ Yeah, yeah, yeah.
come a day when you'll be gone? _____ Whoa. _____
can't de - cide who they should be. _____ Whoa. _____

I un - der - stand _____ a - bout in - de - ci - sion, _____ but

I don't care _____ if I get be - hind. _____

PENNIES FROM HEAVEN
from PENNIES FROM HEAVEN

Words by JOHN BURKE
Music by ARTHUR JOHNSTON

Ev-'ry time it rains it rains pen-nies from heav - en. _____

Don't you know each cloud con - tains pen-nies from heav - en? _____

You'll find your for - tune fall - ing all o - ver town.

Be sure that your um - brel - la is up - side - down.

Trade them for a pack - age of sun - shine and flow - ers. _____

If you want the things you love, you must have show - ers. _____

So when you hear it thun - der, don't run un - der a tree, _____ there'll be

pen - nies from heav - en for you and me. _____

PISTOL PACKIN' MAMA

Words and Music by
AL DEXTER

Bright Country

G

1. Drink - in' beer in a cab - a - ret, ___ and was I hav - in'
2. She kicked out my wind - shield, ___ she hit me o - ver the
3.–6. *(See additional lyrics)*

D7

fun! Un - til one night she caught me right, ___ and
head. She cussed and cried, and said I'd lied, ___ and

G   **Chorus**

now I'm on the run.)
wished that I was dead.)   Lay that pis - tol

down, babe, lay that pis - tol down. **D7** Pis - tol Pack - in'

1–5 **G**	6 **G**

Ma - ma, lay that pis - tol down! down!

Additional Lyrics

3. Drinkin' beer in a cabaret,
   And dancing with a blonde,
   Until one night she shot out the light,
   Bang! That blonde was gone.
   (To Chorus)

4. I'll see you ev'ry night, babe,
   I'll woo you ev'ry day.
   I'll be your regular daddy
   If you'll put that gun away.
   (To Chorus)

5. Drinkin' beer in a cabaret,
   And was I havin' fun!
   Until one night she caught me right,
   And now I'm on the run.
   (To Chorus)

6. Now there was old Al Dexter,
   He always had his fun,
   But with some lead, she shot him dead.
   His honkin' days were done…
   (Chorus to last ending)

A PRETTY GIRL IS LIKE A MELODY
from the 1919 Stage Production ZIEGFELD FOLLIES

Words and Music by
IRVING BERLIN

PUT A LITTLE LOVE IN YOUR HEART

Words and Music by JIMMY HOLIDAY,
RANDY MYERS and JACKIE DeSHANNON

Moderately

Think of your fel - low man, lend him a help - ing hand.
An - oth - er day goes by, and still the chil - dren cry.

Put a lit - tle love in your heart.
Put a lit - tle love in your heart. If

You see, it's get - ting late, oh, please don't hes - i - tate.
you want the world to know, we won't let ha - tred grow.

Put a lit - tle love in your heart.
Put a lit - tle love in your heart. And the world

will be a bet - ter place. And the world

will be a bet - ter place for you and

1.

me. You just wait and see.

PUT YOUR HEAD ON MY SHOULDER

Words and Music by
PAUL ANKA

THE RAINBOW CONNECTION
from THE MUPPET MOVIE

Words and Music by PAUL WILLIAMS
and KENNETH L. ASCHER

Moderately, with a lilt

1. Why are there so man-y songs a-bout rain-bows, and
2. Who said that ev-'ry wish would be heard and an-swered when
3. *(See additional lyrics)*

what's on the oth-er side? _____
wished on the morn-ing star? _____

Rain-bows are vi-sions, ___ but on-ly il-lu-sions, and
Some-bod-y thought of that, and some-one be-lieved it;

rain-bows have noth-ing to hide. _____
look what it's done ___ so far. _____

So we've been told, and some choose to be-lieve it,
What's so a-maz-ing that keeps us star-gaz-ing, and

I know they're wrong, wait and see. _____
what do we think we might see? _____

Am | D C/D | Bm | E7

Some - day we'll find it, the rain - bow con - nec - tion; the
Some - day we'll find it, the rain - bow con - nec - tion; the

Am | D7 | To Coda | 1. G C/G G C/G

lov - ers, the dream - ers and me.
lov - ers, the dream - ers and

2. G | D/F♯ | Em | G/D

me. All of us un - der its spell, we

D.C. al Coda

C | G/B | C/D | D7

know that it's prob - a - bly mag - ic.

CODA

G | D/F♯ | Em | G/D

me. La da da dee da da do la

C | D7 | G

la da da da dee da do. _____

Additional Lyrics

3. Have you been half asleep and have you heard voices?
I've heard them calling my name.
Is this the sweet sound that calls the young sailors?
The voice might be one and the same.
I've heard it too many times to ignore it.
It's something that I'm s'posed to be.
Someday we'll find it,
The rainbow connection;
The lovers, the dreamers and me.

RAINY DAYS AND MONDAYS

Lyrics by PAUL WILLIAMS
Music by ROGER NICHOLS

Moderately slow

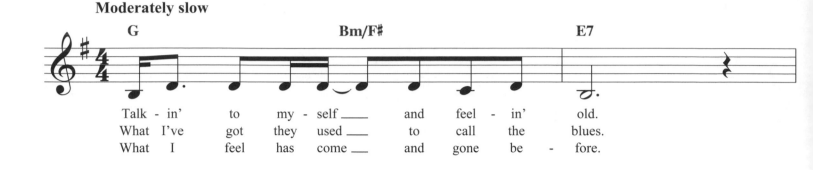

Talk - in' to my - self ____ and feel - in' old.
What I've got they used ____ to call the blues.
What I feel has come ____ and gone be - fore.

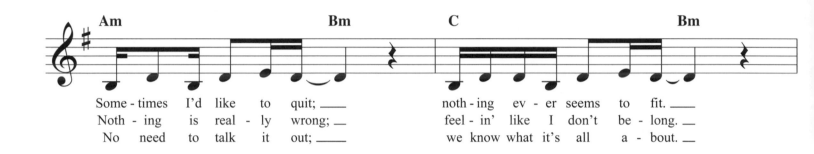

Some - times I'd like to quit; ____ noth - ing ev - er seems to fit. ____
Noth - ing is real - ly wrong; ____ feel - in' like I don't be - long. ____
No need to talk it out; ____ we know what it's all a - bout. ____

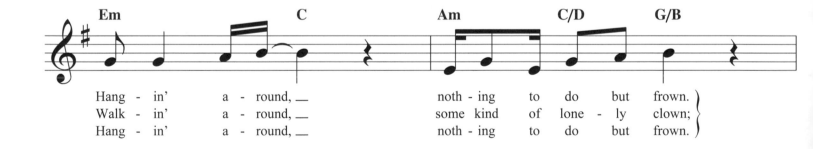

Hang - in' a - round, ____ noth - ing to do but frown.
Walk - in' a - round, ____ some kind of lone - ly clown;
Hang - in' a - round, ____ noth - ing to do but frown.

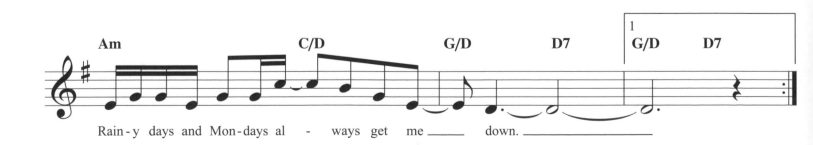

Rain - y days and Mon - days al - ways get me ____ down. ____

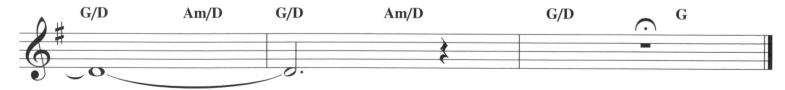

RAMBLIN' ROSE

Words and Music by NOEL SHERMAN
and JOE SHERMAN

Slowly, with a beat

D7			G		
Ram - blin'	Rose, _____	Ram - blin'	Rose, _____		why you
on, _____		ram - ble	on. _____		When your
Rose, _____		Ram - blin'	Rose, _____		why I

A7			D7	G7	C	
ram - ble _____	no one	knows. _____	Wild and	wind - blown, ___
ram - blin' _____	days are	gone, _____	who will	love you ___
want you, _____	heav - en	knows. _____	Though I	love you ___

	G			D7		
_____ that's how	you've	grown, _____	who can	cling	to _____	a Ram - blin'
_____ with a	love	true, _____	when your	ram - blin' _____	days are
_____ with a	love	true, _____	who can	cling	to _____	a Ram - blin'

1, 2

G	C	G	3	G
Rose? _____	Ram - ble	Rose? _____		
gone? _____	Ram - blin'			

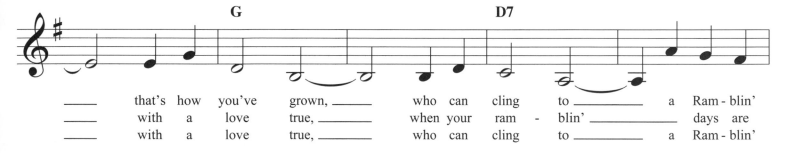
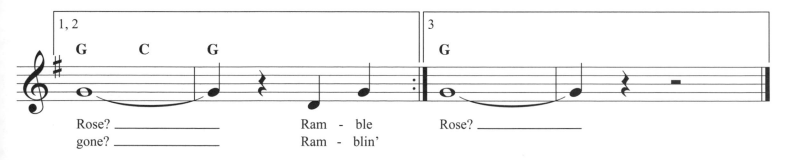

RESPECT

Words and Music by
OTIS REDDING

Moderate Rock

What   you   want,   ba - by,   I   got.
I   ain't gon - na do   you   wrong   while   you   gone.

What   you   need,   you   know   I   got   it.
I   ain't gon - na do   you   wrong   'cause   I   don't   wan - na.

All   I'm   ask - in'   is   for   a   lit - tle   re -

spect   when you come home.   Ba   -   by,   when   you   come   home, __

__   re - spect.   I'm   out __   to   give   you
                                                                Ooh, _____   your   kiss - es,

REVOLUTION

Words and Music by JOHN LENNON
and PAUL McCARTNEY

Moderate Rock 'n' Roll Shuffle

145

SAVE THE BEST FOR LAST

Words and Music by WENDY WALDMAN,
PHIL GALDSTON and JON LIND

(I Never Promised You A)
ROSE GARDEN

Words and Music by
JOE SOUTH

SHOW ME THE WAY

Words and Music by
PETER FRAMPTON

SOUTHERN CROSS

Words and Music by STEPHEN STILLS,
RICHARD CURTIS and MICHAEL CURTIS

SILHOUETTES

Words and Music by FRANK C. SLAY JR.
and BOB CREWE

159

SINGING THE BLUES

Words and Music by
MELVIN ENDSLEY

SIXTEEN CANDLES

Words and Music by LUTHER DIXON
and ALLYSON KHENT

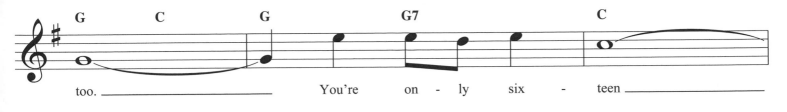

too._____ You're on - ly six - teen _____

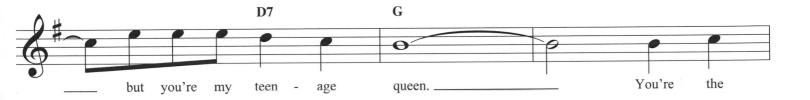

_____ but you're my teen - age queen._____ You're the

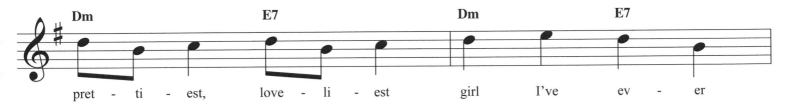

pret - ti - est, love - li - est girl I've ev - er

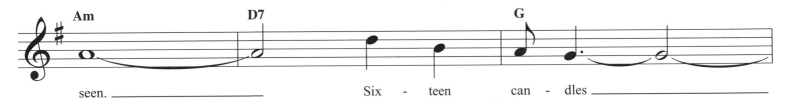

seen._____ Six - teen can - dles _____

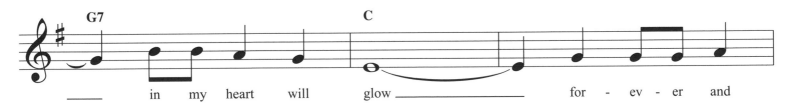

_____ in my heart will glow _____ for - ev - er and

ev - er _____ for I love you so. _____

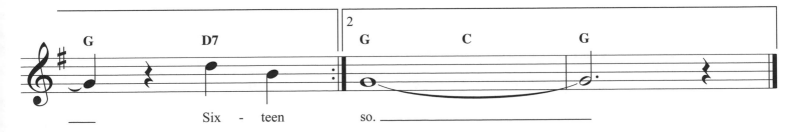

___ Six - teen so. _____

SO NICE
(Summer Samba)

Original Words and Music by MARCOS VALLE
and PAULO SERGIO VALLE
English Words by NORMAN GIMBEL

SOMEWHERE, MY LOVE
Lara's Theme from DOCTOR ZHIVAGO

Lyric by PAUL FRANCIS WEBSTER
Music by MAURICE JARRE

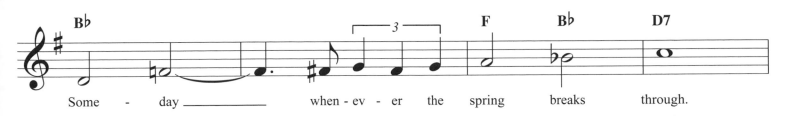

Some - day _____ when - ev - er the spring breaks through.

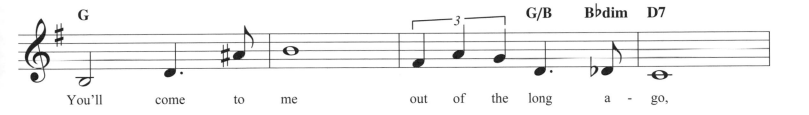

You'll come to me out of the long a - go,

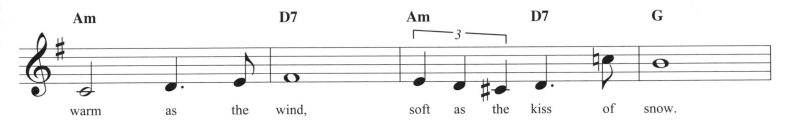

warm as the wind, soft as the kiss of snow.

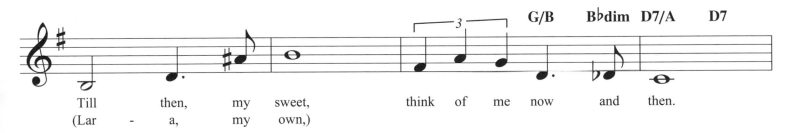

Till then, my sweet, think of me now and then.
(Lar - a, my own,)

God - speed, my love, 'til you are mine a - gain.

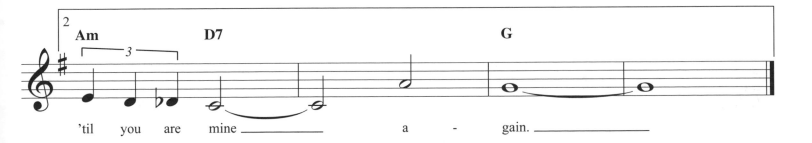

'til you are mine _____ a - gain. _____

SPANISH EYES

Words by CHARLES SINGLETON and EDDIE SNYDER
Music by BERT KAEMPFERT

bring - ing you all the love your heart can

hold. _____ Please _____ say sí

sí, _____ say you and your Span - ish

eyes will wait for me. _____

Span - ish eyes, _____ wait for me, say sí

sí. _____

(Just Like)
STARTING OVER

Words and Music by
JOHN LENNON

172

Our ___ life ___ to -

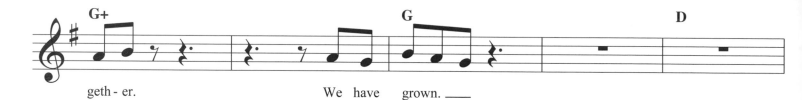

geth - er is so pre - cious to -

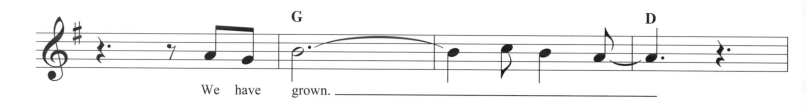

geth - er. We have grown. ___

We have grown. ___

Al - though our love is still spe - cial,

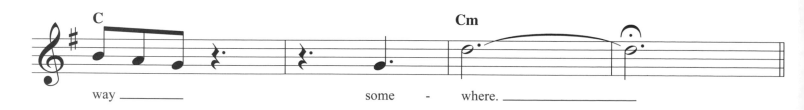

let's take ___ a chance and ___ fly a -

way ___ some - where. ___

(Instrumental)

A SPOONFUL OF SUGAR
from Walt Disney's MARY POPPINS

Words and Music by RICHARD M. SHERMAN
and ROBERT B. SHERMAN

In ev-'ry job that must be done there is an el-e-ment of fun; you
feath-er-ing his nest has ver-y lit-tle time to rest while
bees that fetch the nec-tar from the flow-ers to the comb nev-er

find the fun and snap! the job's a game; ____ and ev-'ry task you un-der-
gath-er-ing his bits of twine and twig. ____ Though quite in-tent in his pur-
tire of ev-er buzz-ing to and fro. ____ Be-cause they take a lit-tle

take be-comes a piece of cake, a lark! A spree! It's
suit he has a mer-ry tune to toot; he knows a song will
nip from ev-'ry flow-er that they sip, and hence, they find their

ver-y clear to see that
move the job a-long. For a spoon-ful of sug-ar helps the med-i-cine go
task is not a grind. For

down, the med-i-cine go down, ____ med-i-cine go down. Just a

spoon-ful of sug-ar helps the med-i-cine go down in a most de-

light-ful way.   A rob-in
                                   The hon-ey   way. ____

STILL THE SAME

Words and Music by
BOB SEGER

Moderately, with a beat

G

You al - ways won, ____ ev - 'ry time you placed a bet. ____
al - ways said ____ the cards would nev - er do you wrong. ____

Instrumental

Bm   **D**   **G**

____ You're still damn good; ____
____ The trick, you said, ____ was

Bm   **D**

no one's got - ten to you yet. _____
nev - er play the game too long. ____

A

End instrumental

C   **D**

Ev - 'ry time ____ they were sure they had you caught, ____
gam - bler's share; ____ the on - ly risk that you would take, ____
There you stood; ____ ev - 'ry - bod - y watched you play. ____

G   **B**

____ you were quick - er than they thought. ____
____ the on - ly loss you could for - sake, ____
____ I just turned and walked a - way. ____

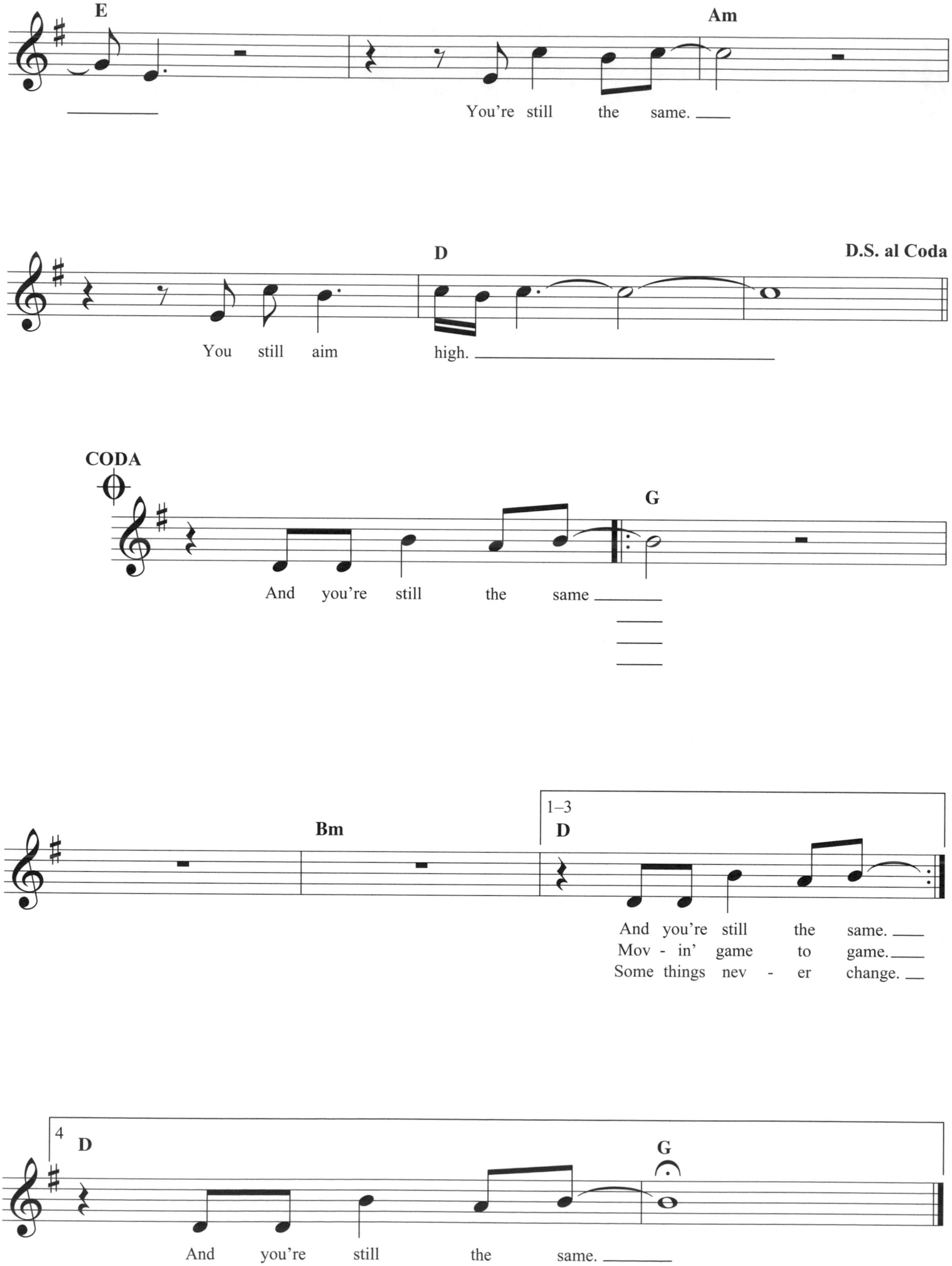
E
Am
You're still the same.
D
D.S. al Coda
You still aim high.
CODA
G
And you're still the same
Bm
1–3
D
And you're still the same.
Mov - in' game to game.
Some things nev - er change.
4
D
G
And you're still the same.

STORMY WEATHER
(Keeps Rainin' All the Time)
from COTTON CLUB PARADE OF 1933

Lyric by TED KOEHLER
Music by HAROLD ARLEN

SUGARTIME

Words and Music by CHARLES PHILLIPS
and ODIS ECHOLS

SUNDOWN

Words and Music by
GORDON LIGHTFOOT

Moderately

1. I can see her ly-ing back in her sat-in dress ___ in a
2.–4. *(See additional lyrics)*

room where you do ___ what you don't con-fess. ___

Sun-down, you bet-ter take care ___ if I

find you been creep-ing 'round ___ my back stairs. ___

Sun-down, you bet-ter take care ___ if I

find you been creep-ing 'round ___ my back stairs. ___

Additional Lyrics

2. She's been looking like a queen in a sailor's dream,
   And she don't always say what she really means.
   Sometimes I think it's a shame when I get feeling better when I'm feeling no pain.
   Sometimes I think it's a shame when I get feeling better when I'm feeling no pain.

3. I can picture ev'ry move that a man could make.
   Getting lost in her loving is your first mistake.
   Sundown, you better take care if I find you been creeping 'round my back stairs.
   Sometimes I think it's a sin when I feel like I'm winning when I'm losing again.

4. I can see her looking fast in her faded jeans.
   She's a hard-loving woman, got me feeling mean.
   Sometimes I think it's a shame when I get feeling better when I'm feeling no pain.
   Sundown, you better take care if I find you been creeping 'round my back stairs.

THE SURREY WITH THE FRINGE ON TOP
from OKLAHOMA!

Lyrics by OSCAR HAMMERSTEIN II
Music by RICHARD RODGERS

TEARS ON MY PILLOW

Words and Music by SYLVESTER BRADFORD
and AL LEWIS

TEQUILA

By CHUCK RIO

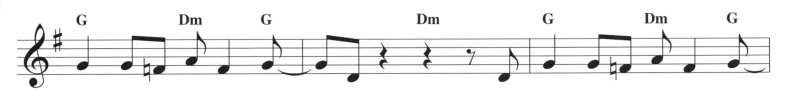

(Spoken:) Tequila!

(Spoken:) Tequila!

TAKE MY BREATH AWAY
(Love Theme)
from the Paramount Picture TOP GUN

Words and Music by GIORGIO MORODER
and TOM WHITLOCK

Moderately slow

1. Watch-ing ev-ery mo-tion in _____ my fool-ish lov-er's game; _____
2., 3. *(See additional lyrics)*

(Instrumental) on this end-less o-cean, fi - n'lly lov-ers know no shame. _____

_____ Turn - ing and re-turn - ing to _____

_____ some se-cret place in - side; _____

watch-ing in slow mo-tion as _____ you turn a-round and say,

"Take my breath a - way." _____ *(Instrumental)*

"Take my breath a - way." _____ (Instrumental)

Through the hour - glass I saw _____ you. In time _____ you slipped a - way. _____

Bridge

When the mir - ror crashed, I called ___ you and turned ___ to hear you say, "If on - ly for to - day _____ I _____ am un - a-

fraid. _____ Take my breath a - way." _____ (Instrumental)

"Take my breath a -

CODA

_____ My love, ___ take my breath a - way. _____ (Instrumental)

My love, ___ take my breath a -

Additional Lyrics

2. Watching, I keep waiting, still anticipating love,
   Never hesitating to become the fated ones.
   Turning and returning to some secret place to hide;
   Watching in slow motion as you turn to me and say,
   "Take my breath away."
   (To Bridge)

3. Watching every motion in this foolish lover's game;
   Haunted by the notion somewhere there's a love in flames.
   Turning and returning to some secret place inside;
   Watching in slow motion as you turn my way and say,
   "Take my breath away."
   (To Coda)

THAT'LL BE THE DAY

Words and Music by JERRY ALLISON,
NORMAN PETTY and BUDDY HOLLY

THERE'S A KIND OF HUSH
(All Over the World)

Words and Music by LES REED
and GEOFF STEPHENS

Medium tempo, with a beat

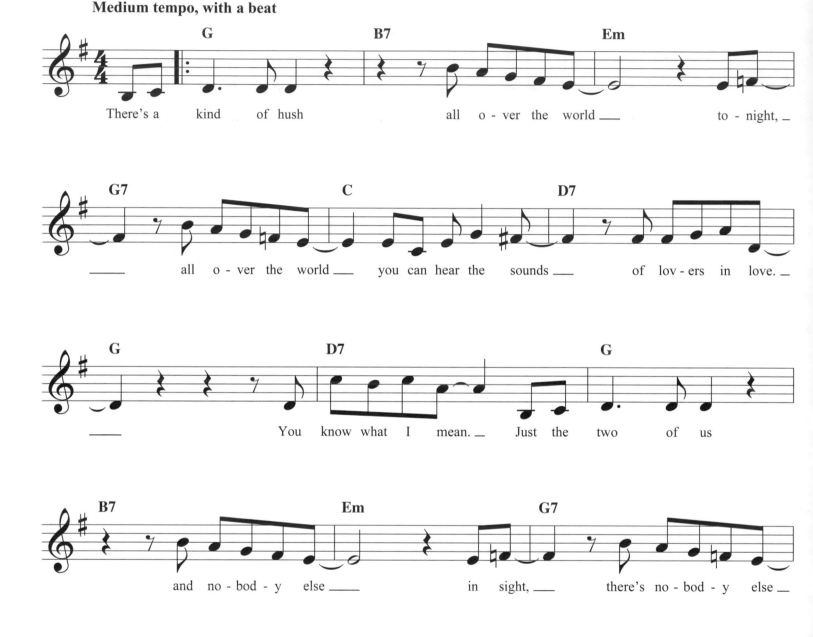

There's a kind of hush all o - ver the world to - night, all o - ver the world you can hear the sounds of lov - ers in love.

You know what I mean. Just the two of us and no - bod - y else in sight, there's no - bod - y else and I'm feel - ing good just hold - ing you tight. So

lis - ten ver - y care - ful - ly, clos - er now and you

THE TIMES THEY ARE A-CHANGIN'

Words and Music by
BOB DYLAN

1. Come gath - er 'round peo - ple wher - ev - er you roam _____
2.–5. *(See additional lyrics)*

_____ and ad - mit that the wa - ters a - round you have

grown. And ac - cept it that soon you'll be drenched to the

bone, _____ if your time to you is worth

sav - in' _____ then you bet - ter start swim - min' or you'll

sink like a stone, for the times they are a -

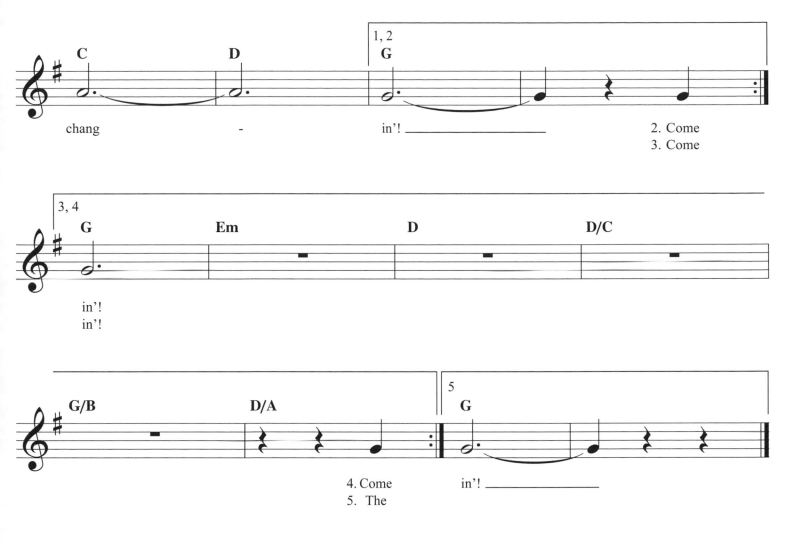

chang - in'! _____ 2. Come
3. Come

in'!
in'!

4. Come in'! _____
5. The

Additional Lyrics

2. Come writers and critics
Who prophesy with your pen
And keep your eyes wide
The chance won't come again.
And don't speak too soon
For the wheel's still in spin,
And there's no tellin' who
That it's namin'.
For the loser now
Will be later to win
For the times they are a-changin'.

3. Come senators, congressmen
Please heed the call
Don't stand in the doorway
Don't block up the hall.
For he that gets hurt
Will be he who has stalled,
There's a battle
Outside and it's ragin'.
It'll soon shake your windows
And rattle your walls
For the times they are a-changin'!

4. Come mothers and fathers
Throughout the land,
And don't criticize
What you can't understand.
Your sons and your daughters
Are beyond your command,
Your old road is
Rapidly agin'.
Please get out of the new one
If you can't lend your hand
For the times they are a-changin'!

5. The line it is drawn
The curse it is cast
The slow one now will
Later be fast.
As the present now
Will later be past,
The order is rapidly fadin'.
And the first one now
Will later be last
For the times they are a-changin'!

THE TWIST

Words and Music by
HANK BALLARD

Additional Lyrics

2. While daddy is sleeping and mama ain't around,
   While daddy is sleeping and mama ain't around,
   We're gonna twisty, twisty, twisty until we tear the house down.
   Chorus

3. You should see my little sis.
   You should see my little sis.
   She knows how to rock and she knows how to twist.
   Chorus

WHEN I NEED YOU

Words and Music by CAROLE BAYER SAGER
and ALBERT HAMMOND

When I need you, I just close my eyes and I'm

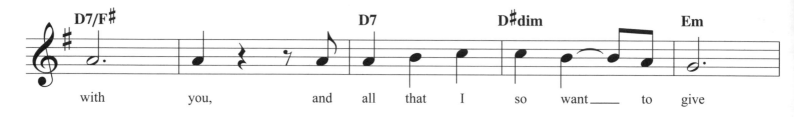

with you, and all that I so want to give

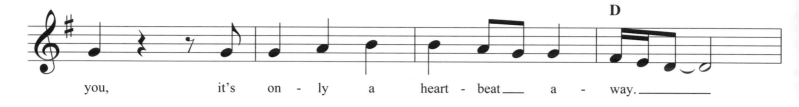

you, it's on-ly a heart-beat a-way.

When I need love, I hold out my hands and I

touch love, I nev-er knew there was so much love

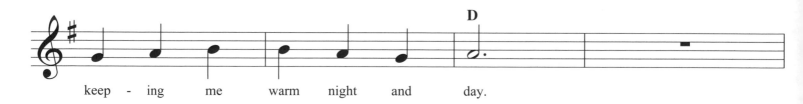

keep-ing me warm night and day.

Miles and miles of emp-ty space in be-tween us,
It's not eas-y when the road is your driv-er,
a

A WHOLE NEW WORLD
from Disney ALADDIN

Music by ALAN MENKEN
Lyrics by TIM RICE

YOU ARE THE SUNSHINE OF MY LIFE

Words and Music by
STEVIE WONDER

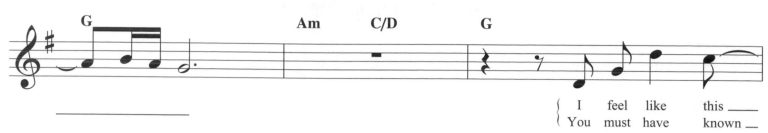

I feel like this _____
You must have known _____

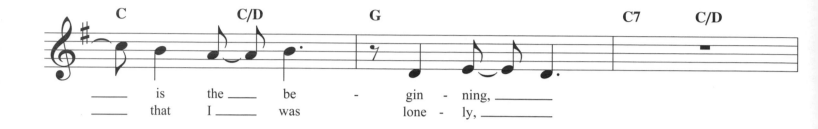

_____ is the _____ be - gin - ning, _____
_____ that I _____ was lone - ly, _____

though I've loved you _____ for a mil - lion years. _____
be - cause you came _____ to my res - cue. _____

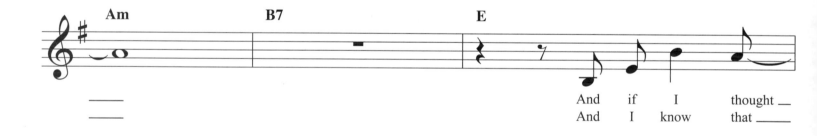

And if I thought _____
And I know that _____

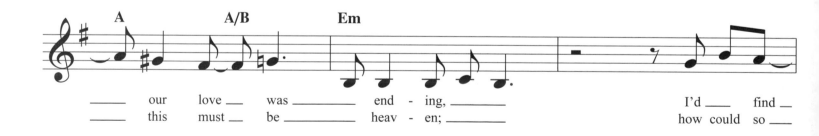

_____ our love _____ was _____ end - ing, _____ I'd _____ find _____
_____ this must _____ be _____ heav - en; _____ how could so _____

_____ my - self _____ drown - ing in my _____ own
_____ much love _____ be _____ in - side _____ of

tears.   Whoa. _____
you?   Whoa. _____   You are the sun -

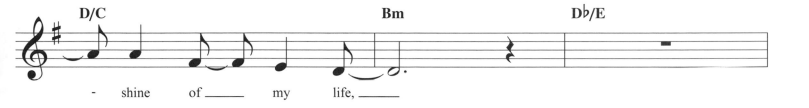

- shine of _____ my life, _____

that's why I'll al - ways { be _____ / stay _____ } a - round. _____

You are the ap - ple of ____ my eye. ___

_____ For - ev - er you'll __

Repeat and Fade

_____ stay in _____ my heart. _____

WHY DO FOOLS FALL IN LOVE

Words and Music by MORRIS LEVY
and FRANKIE LYMON

WONDERFUL TONIGHT

Words and Music by
ERIC CLAPTON

_____

I feel won - der - ful _____ be -

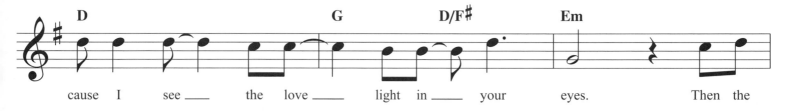

cause I see _____ the love _____ light in _____ your eyes. Then the

won - der of it all _____ is that you just don't _ re - al - ize _

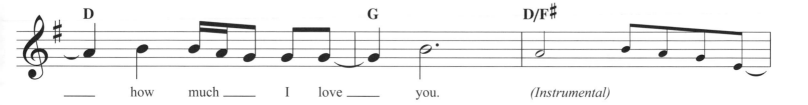

_____ how much _____ I love _____ you. *(Instrumental)*

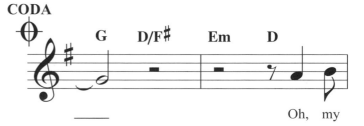

_____ Oh, my

dar - ling, you are won - der - ful _____ to - night." _

YOU LIGHT UP MY LIFE

Words and Music by
JOSEPH BROOKS

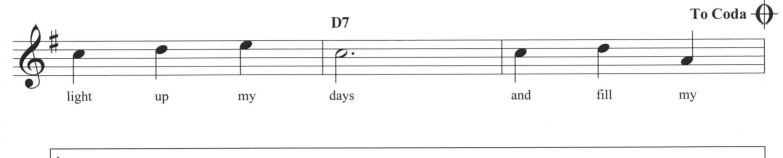

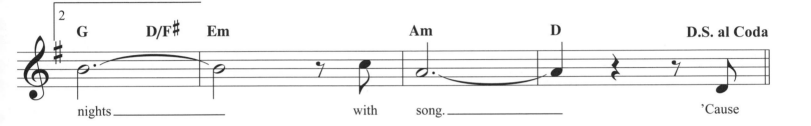

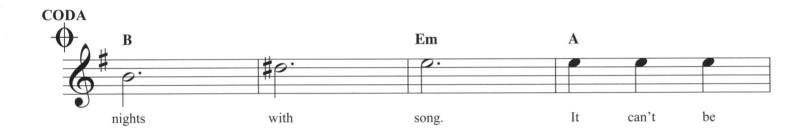

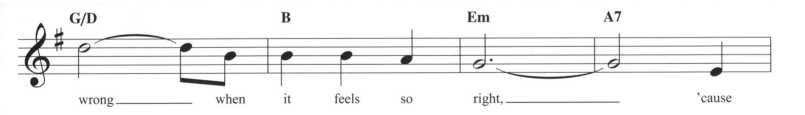

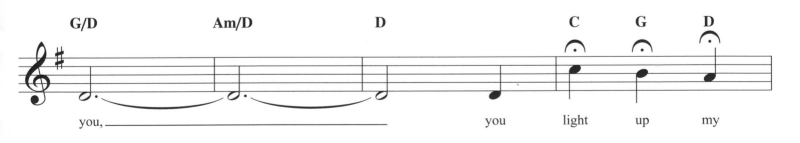

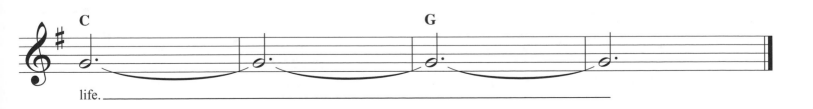

YOU'RE STILL THE ONE

Words and Music by SHANIA TWAIN
and R.J. LANGE

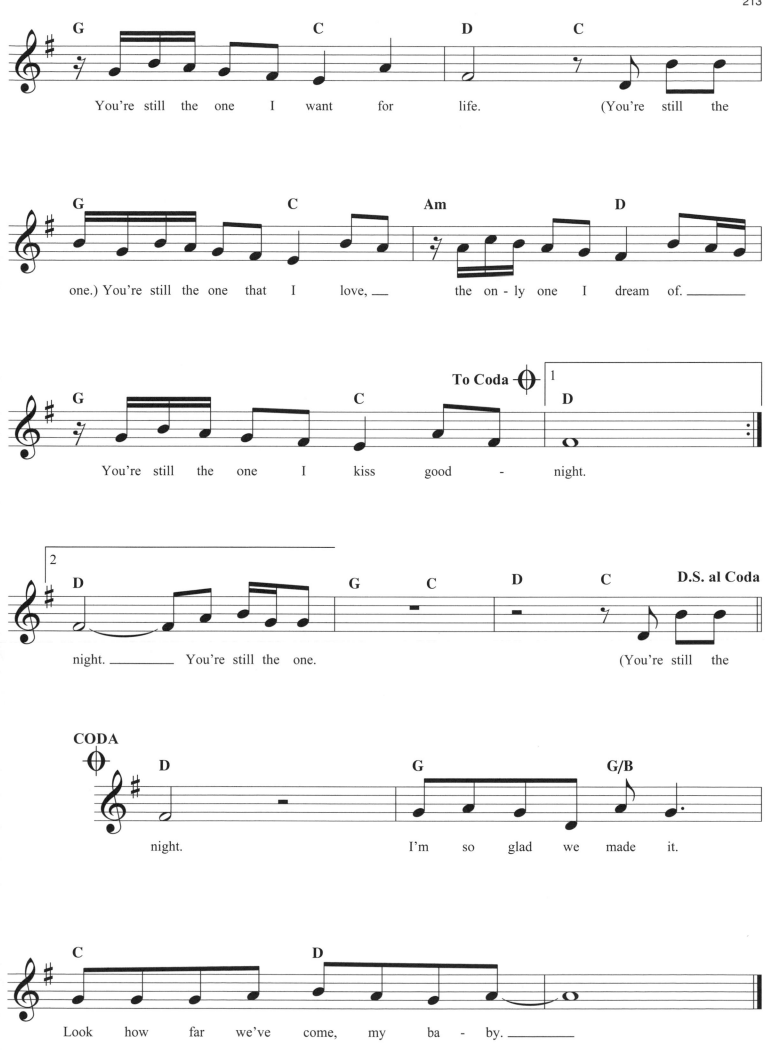

CHORD SPELLER

C chords

C	C–E–G
Cm	C–E♭–G
C7	C–E–G–B♭
Cdim	C–E♭–G♭
C+	C–E–G♯

C♯ or D♭ chords

C♯	C♯–F–G♯
C♯m	C♯–E–G♯
C♯7	C♯–F– G♯–B
C♯dim	C♯–E–G
C♯+	C♯–F–A

D chords

D	D–F♯–A
Dm	D–F–A
D7	D–F♯–A–C
Ddim	D–F–A♭
D+	D–F♯–A♯

E♭ chords

E♭	E♭–G–B♭
E♭m	E♭–G♭–B♭
E♭7	E♭–G–B♭–D♭
E♭dim	E♭–G♭–A
E♭+	E♭–G–B

E chords

E	E–G♯–B
Em	E–G–B
E7	E–G♯–B–D
Edim	E–G–B♭
E+	E–G♯–C

F chords

F	F–A–C
Fm	F–A♭–C
F7	F–A–C–E♭
Fdim	F–A♭–B
F+	F–A–C♯

F♯ or G♭ chords

F♯	F♯–A♯–C♯
F♯m	F♯–A–C♯
F♯7	F♯–A♯–C♯–E
F♯dim	F♯–A–C
F♯+	F♯–A♯–D

G chords

G	G–B–D
Gm	G–B♭–D
G7	G–B–D–F
Gdim	G–B♭–D♭
G+	G–B–D♯

G♯ or A♭ chords

A♭	A♭–C–E♭
A♭m	A♭–B–E♭
A♭7	A♭–C–E♭–G♭
A♭dim	A♭–B–D
A♭+	A♭–C–E

A chords

A	A–C♯–E
Am	A–C–E
A7	A–C♯–E–G
Adim	A–C–E♭
A+	A–C♯–F

B♭ chords

B♭	B♭–D–F
B♭m	B♭–D♭–F
B♭7	B♭–D–F–A♭
B♭dim	B♭–D♭–E
B♭+	B♭–D–F♯

B chords

B	B–D♯–F♯
Bm	B–D–F♯
B7	B–D♯–F♯–A
Bdim	B–D–F
B+	B–D♯–G

Important Note: A slash chord (C/E, G/B) tells you that a certain bass note is to be played under a particular harmony. In the case of C/E, the chord is C and the bass note is E.

HAL LEONARD PRESENTS
FAKE BOOKS FOR BEGINNERS!

Entry-level fake books! These books feature larger-than-most fake book notation with simplified harmonies and melodies – and all songs are in the key of C. An introduction addresses basic instruction in playing from a fake book.

YOUR FIRST FAKE BOOK
00240112.............................$19.95

THE EASY FAKE BOOK
00240144.............................$19.95

THE SIMPLIFIED FAKE BOOK
00240168.............................$19.95

THE BEATLES EASY FAKE BOOK
00240309.............................$25.00

THE EASY BROADWAY FAKE BOOK
00240180.............................$19.95

THE EASY CHILDREN'S FAKE BOOK
00240428 ....$19.99

THE EASY CHRISTIAN FAKE BOOK
00240328.............................$19.99

THE EASY CHRISTMAS FAKE BOOK – 2ND EDITION
00240209.............................$19.95

THE EASY CLASSIC ROCK FAKE BOOK
00240389 ....$19.99

THE EASY CLASSICAL FAKE BOOK
00240262.............................$19.95

THE EASY COUNTRY FAKE BOOK
00240319.............................$19.95

THE EASY DISNEY FAKE BOOK
00240551.............................$19.99

THE EASY EARLY SONGS FAKE BOOK
00240337 ....$19.99

THE EASY FOLKSONG FAKE BOOK
00240360.............................$19.99

THE EASY GOSPEL FAKE BOOK
00240169.............................$19.99

THE EASY HYMN FAKE BOOK
00240207.............................$19.95

THE EASY JAZZ STANDARDS FAKE BOOK
00102346.............................$19.99

THE EASY LATIN FAKE BOOK
00240333.............................$19.99

THE EASY MOVIE FAKE BOOK
00240295.............................$19.95

THE EASY SHOW TUNES FAKE BOOK
00240297.............................$19.95

THE EASY STANDARDS FAKE BOOK
00240294.............................$19.95

THE EASY 3-CHORD FAKE BOOK
00240388 ....$19.99

THE EASY WORSHIP FAKE BOOK
00240265.............................$19.95

MORE OF THE EASY WORSHIP FAKE BOOK
00240362 ....$19.99

THE EASY TWENTIES FAKE BOOK
00240336 ....$19.99

THE EASY THIRTIES FAKE BOOK
00240335 ....$19.99

THE EASY FORTIES FAKE BOOK
00240252.............................$19.95

MORE OF THE EASY FORTIES FAKE BOOK
00240287.............................$19.95

THE EASY FIFTIES FAKE BOOK
00240255.............................$19.95

MORE OF THE EASY FIFTIES FAKE BOOK
00240288.............................$19.95

THE EASY SIXTIES FAKE BOOK
00240253.............................$19.95

MORE OF THE EASY SIXTIES FAKE BOOK
00240289.............................$19.95

THE EASY SEVENTIES FAKE BOOK
00240256.............................$19.95

MORE OF THE EASY SEVENTIES FAKE BOOK
00240290.............................$19.95

THE EASY EIGHTIES FAKE BOOK
00240340 ....$19.99

THE EASY NINETIES FAKE BOOK
00240341 ....$19.99

FOR MORE INFORMATION, SEE YOUR LOCAL MUSIC DEALER, OR WRITE TO:

HAL•LEONARD®
CORPORATION
7777 W. BLUEMOUND RD. P.O. BOX 13819 MILWAUKEE, WI 53213

www.halleonard.com

0215

Prices, contents and availability subject to change without notice.

THE ULTIMATE COLLECTION OF
FAKE BOOKS

The Real Book – Sixth Edition

Hal Leonard proudly presents the first legitimate and legal editions of these books ever produced. These bestselling titles are mandatory for anyone who plays jazz! Over 400 songs, including: All By Myself • Dream a Little Dream of Me • God Bless the Child • Like Someone in Love • When I Fall in Love • and more.

00240221 Volume 1, C Edition.................$35.00
00240224 Volume 1, B♭ Edition...............$35.00
00240225 Volume 1, E♭ Edition...............$35.00
00240226 Volume 1, BC Edition...............$35.00
00240222 Volume 2, C Edition.................$35.00
00240227 Volume 2, B♭ Edition...............$35.00
00240228 Volume 2, E♭ Edition...............$35.00

Best Fake Book Ever – 4th Edition

More than 1,000 songs from all styles of music, including: All My Loving • At the Hop • Cabaret • Dust in the Wind • Fever • From a Distance • Hello, Dolly! • Hey Jude • King of the Road • Longer • Misty • Route 66 • Sentimental Journey • Somebody • Song Sung Blue • Spinning Wheel • Unchained Melody • We Will Rock You • What a Wonderful World • Wooly Bully • Y.M.C.A. • and more.

00290239 C Edition $49.99
00240083 B♭ Edition $49.95
00240084 E♭ Edition $49.95

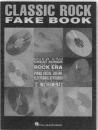

Classic Rock Fake Book – 2nd Edition

This fake book is a great compilation of more than 250 terrific songs of the rock era, arranged for piano, voice, guitar and all C instruments. Includes: All Right Now • American Woman • Birthday • Honesty • I Shot the Sheriff • I Want You to Want Me • Imagine • It's Still Rock and Roll to Me • Lay Down Sally • Layla • My Generation • Rock and Roll All Nite • Spinning Wheel • White Room • We Will Rock You • lots more!
00240108 ....$32.50

Classical Fake Book – 2nd Edition

This unprecedented, amazingly comprehensive reference includes over 850 classical themes and melodies for all classical music lovers. Includes everything from Renaissance music to Vivaldi and Mozart to Mendelssohn. Lyrics in the original language are included when appropriate.
00240044 ....$37.50

The Disney Fake Book – 3rd Edition

Over 200 of the most beloved songs of all time, including: Be Our Guest • Can You Feel the Love Tonight • Colors of the Wind • Cruella De Vil • Friend Like Me • Heigh-Ho • It's a Small World • Mickey Mouse March • Supercalifragilisticexpialidocious • Under the Sea • When You Wish upon a Star • A Whole New World • Zip-A-Dee-Doo-Dah • and more!
00240039 ....$30.00

(Disney characters and artwork © Disney Enterprises, Inc.)

The Folksong Fake Book

Over 1,000 folksongs perfect for performers, school teachers, and hobbyists. Includes: Bury Me Not on the Lone Prairie • Clementine • Danny Boy • The Erie Canal • Go, Tell It on the Mountain • Home on the Range • Kumbaya • Michael Row the Boat Ashore • Shenandoah • Simple Gifts • Swing Low, Sweet Chariot • When Johnny Comes Marching Home • Yankee Doodle • and many more.
00240151 ....$24.95

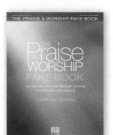

The Hymn Fake Book

Nearly 1,000 multi-denominational hymns perfect for church musicians or hobbyists: Amazing Grace • Christ the Lord Is Risen Today • For the Beauty of the Earth • It Is Well with My Soul • A Mighty Fortress Is Our God • O for a Thousand Tongues to Sing • Praise to the Lord, the Almighty • Take My Life and Let It Be • What a Friend We Have in Jesus • and hundreds more!
00240145 ....$24.95

The Praise & Worship Fake Book

400 songs: As the Deer • Better Is One Day • Come, Now Is the Time to Worship • Firm Foundation • Glorify Thy Name • Here I Am to Worship • I Could Sing of Your Love Forever • Lord, I Lift Your Name on High • More Precious Than Silver • Open the Eyes of My Heart • The Power of Your Love • Shine, Jesus, Shine • Trading My Sorrows • We Fall Down • You Are My All in All • and more.
00240234...$34.95

The R&B Fake Book – 2nd Edition

This terrific fake book features 375 classic R&B hits: Baby Love • Best of My Love • Dancing in the Street • Easy • Get Ready • Heatwave • Here and Now • Just Once • Let's Get It On • The Loco-Motion • (You Make Me Feel Like) A Natural Woman • One Sweet Day • Papa Was a Rollin' Stone • Save the Best for Last • September • Sexual Healing • Shop Around • Still • Tell It Like It Is • Up on the Roof • Walk on By • What's Going On • more!
00240107 C Edition $29.95

Ultimate Broadway Fake Book – 5th Edition

More than 700 show-stoppers from over 200 shows! Includes: Ain't Misbehavin' • All I Ask of You • Bewitched • Camelot • Don't Cry for Me Argentina • Edelweiss • I Dreamed a Dream • If I Were a Rich Man • Memory • Oklahoma • Send in the Clowns • What I Did for Love • more.
00240046...$49.99

The Ultimate Christmas Fake Book – 5th Edition

This updated edition includes 275 traditional and contemporary Christmas songs: Away in a Manger • The Christmas Song • Deck the Hall • Frosty the Snow Man • A Holly Jolly Christmas • I Heard the Bells on Christmas Day • Jingle Bells • Little Saint Nick • Merry Christmas, Darling • Nuttin' for Christmas • Rudolph the Red-Nosed Reindeer • Silent Night • What Child Is This? • more.
00240045 ....$24.95

The Ultimate Country Fake Book – 5th Edition

This book includes over 700 of your favorite country hits: Always on My Mind • Boot Scootin' Boogie • Crazy • Down at the Twist and Shout • Forever and Ever, Amen • Friends in Low Places • The Gambler • Jambalaya • King of the Road • Sixteen Tons • There's a Tear in My Beer • Your Cheatin' Heart • and hundreds more.

00240049 ....$49.99

The Ultimate Fake Book – 5th Edition

Includes over 1,200 hits: Blue Skies • Body and Soul • Endless Love • Isn't It Romantic? • Memory • Mona Lisa • Moon River • Operator • Piano Man • Roxanne • Satin Doll • Shout • Small World • Smile • Speak Softly, Love • Strawberry Fields Forever • Tears in Heaven • Unforgettable • hundreds more!

00240024 C Edition $49.95
00240026 B♭ Edition............................$49.95
00240025 E♭ Edition............................$49.95

The Ultimate Pop/Rock Fake Book – 4th Edition

Over 600 pop standards and contemporary hits, including: All Shook Up • Another One Bites the Dust • Crying • Don't Know Much • Dust in the Wind • Earth Angel • Every Breath You Take • Hero • Hey Jude • Hold My Hand • Imagine • Layla • The Loco-Motion • Oh, Pretty Woman • On Broadway • Spinning Wheel • Stand by Me • Stayin' Alive • Tears in Heaven • True Colors • The Twist • Vision of Love • A Whole New World • Wild Thing • Wooly Bully • Yesterday • more!
00240099 ....$39.99

Fake Book of the World's Favorite Songs – 4th Edition

Over 700 favorites, including: America the Beautiful • Anchors Aweigh • Battle Hymn of the Republic • Bill Bailey, Won't You Please Come Home • Chopsticks • Für Elise • His Eye Is on the Sparrow • I Wonder Who's Kissing Her Now • Jesu, Joy of Man's Desiring • My Old Kentucky Home • Sidewalks of New York • Take Me Out to the Ball Game • When the Saints Go Marching In • and hundreds more!
00240072 ....$22.95

FOR MORE INFORMATION, SEE YOUR LOCAL MUSIC DEALER, OR WRITE TO:

HAL•LEONARD®
CORPORATION
7777 W. BLUEMOUND RD. P.O. BOX 13819 MILWAUKEE, WI 53213

Complete songlists available online at
www.halleonard.com

Prices, contents and availabilty subject to change without notice.